TURN THAT LIGHT OUT! HOME LIFE IN WORLD WAR II

written by **Ken Adey**

illustrated by **Kathy Baxendale**

CONTENTS

WAR BEGINS

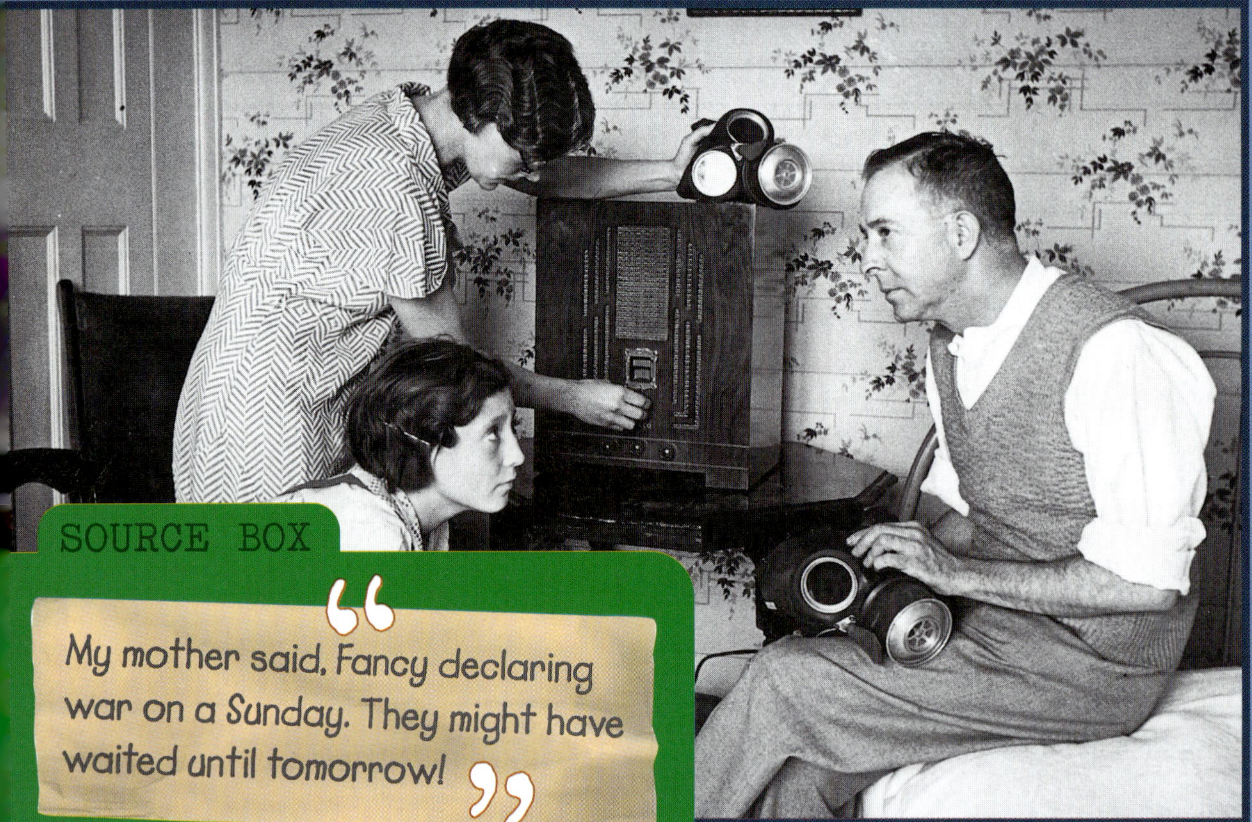

SOURCE BOX

"My mother said, Fancy declaring war on a Sunday. They might have waited until tomorrow!"

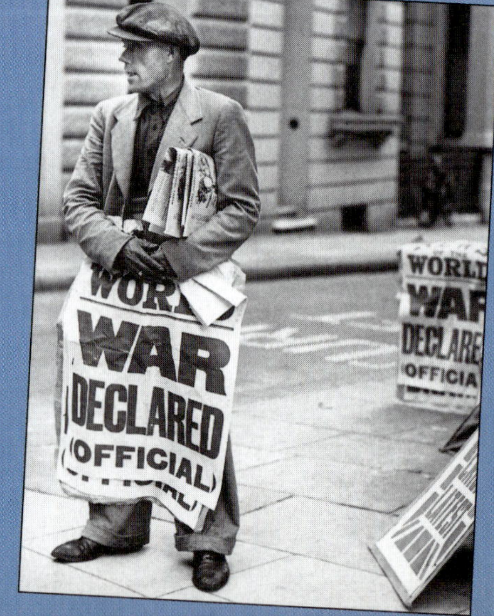

Sunday 3rd September 1939 was a warm sunny day, but few people in Britain were outside in the sunshine. Most were listening to the Prime Minister, Neville Chamberlain, on the radio. "This country is at war with Germany," he announced.

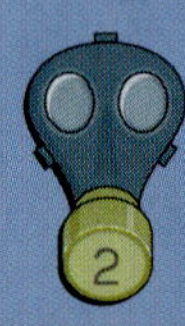

Everybody believed that German planes would come and drop bombs of poisonous gas on the country. Gas masks had been given out even before the war started.

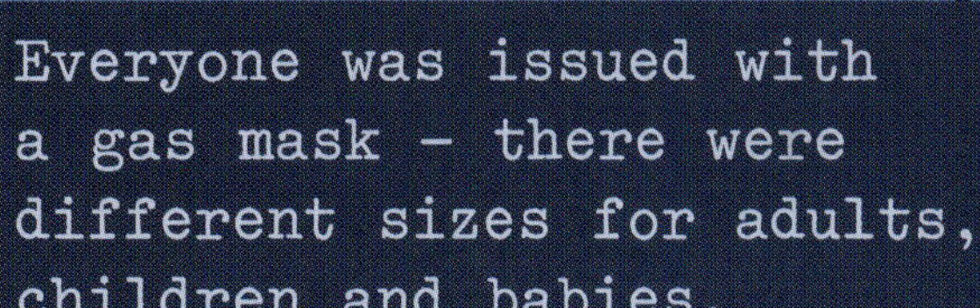

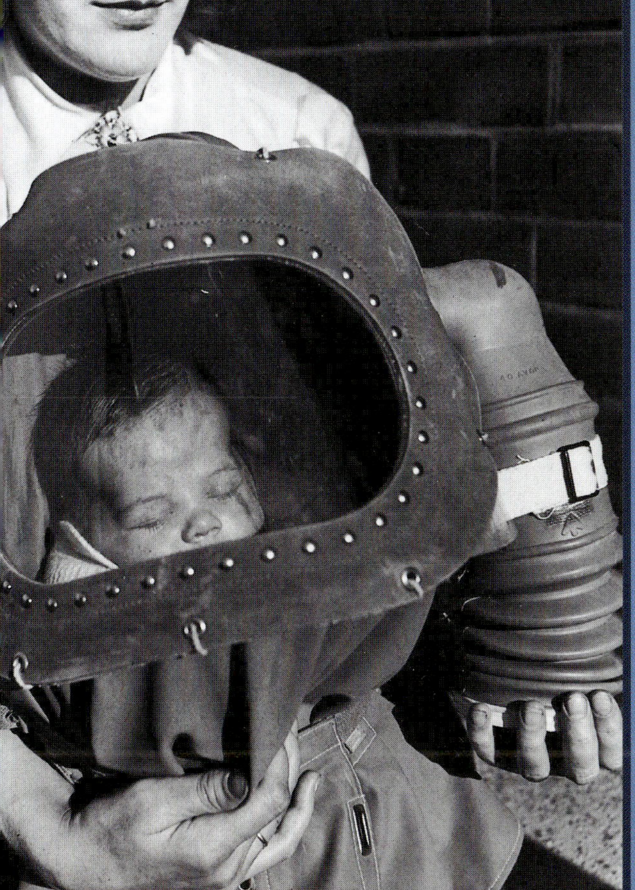

Everyone was issued with a gas mask – there were different sizes for adults, children and babies.

 At school you had to practise putting your mask on quickly. It was not easy because the straps kept getting tangled up.

These blue and red gas masks which children wore were called Mickey Mouse masks because they looked like the famous cartoon character.

SOURCE BOX

"Gas masks must be brought to school and must have the owner's name on the strap as well as on the box."

Life was going to be very different. Your father would probably join the army, navy or air force. He would go off to fight and you would not see him for many months or even years. A lot of men, of course, never came back because they were killed during the war.

"We have known for a long time that war was going to happen sooner or later. I think most people are worried but everybody is trying not to show it. We all want to look brave."

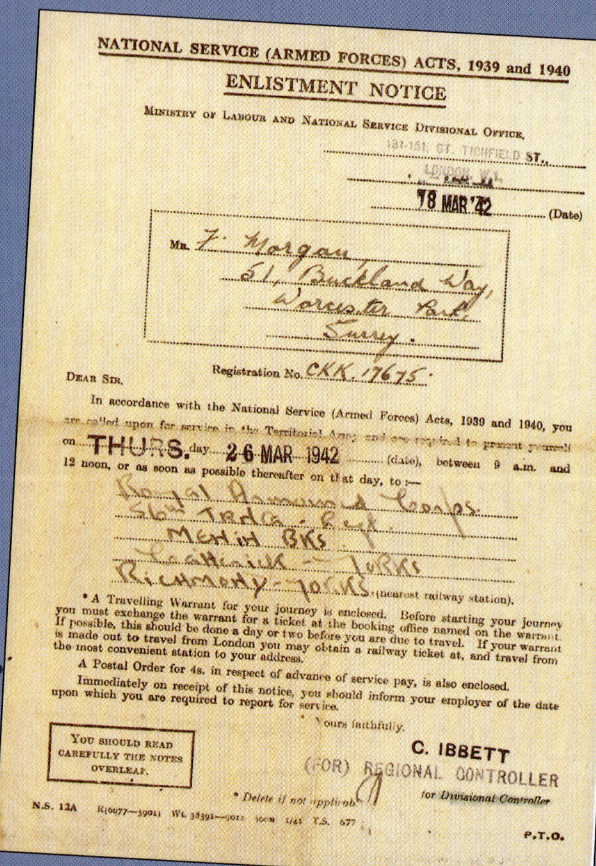

NATIONAL SERVICE (ARMED FORCES) ACTS, 1939 and 1940

ENLISTMENT NOTICE

MINISTRY OF LABOUR AND NATIONAL SERVICE DIVISIONAL OFFICE,

131-151, GT. TICHFIELD ST.,

LONDON, W.1

18 MAR '42 .... (Date)

Mr. F. Morgan
51, Buckland Way,
Worcester Park
Surry.

Registration No. CKK 17675.

DEAR SIR,

In accordance with the National Service (Armed Forces) Acts, 1939 and 1940, you are called upon for service in the Territorial Army, and are required to present yourself on THURS. day 26 MAR 1942 .... (date), between 9 a.m. and 12 noon, or as soon as possible thereafter on that day, to :—

Royal Armoured Corps.
51st Tank Regt.
Menin Bks
Catterick – Yorks
Richmond – Yorks .... (nearest railway station).

* A Travelling Warrant for your journey is enclosed. Before starting your journey you must exchange the warrant for a ticket at the booking office named on the warrant. If possible, this should be done a day or two before you are due to travel. If your warrant is made out to travel from London you may obtain a railway ticket at, and travel from the most convenient station to your address.

A Postal Order for 4s. in respect of advance of service pay, is also enclosed.

Immediately on receipt of this notice, you should inform your employer of the date upon which you are required to report for service.

Yours faithfully,

C. IBBETT
(FOR) REGIONAL CONTROLLER
for Divisional Controller

YOU SHOULD READ CAREFULLY THE NOTES OVERLEAF.

* Delete if not applicable

N.S. 12A   R(9077—5901)   Wt. 38391—9012   500M 1/41 T.S. 677   P.T.O.

Your mother would probably go out to work. Women had to take over the jobs that men had been doing. You might have to leave home and go to live in the country where you would be safer. Even the meals you ate were going to change.

"If an air raid occurs at school the Head Teacher will give the order 'GAS' in each classroom. The children will put on their masks, run on to the school field, and lie down."

What was it like growing up in wartime Britain?

EVACUATION

Because of the fear that large towns and cities would soon be bombed it was decided that children should be evacuated from towns and sent to villages in the countryside. You went by train. You had no idea where you were going, nor did your parents. You had a label with your name and address attached to your coat, or hanging from a piece of string round your neck.

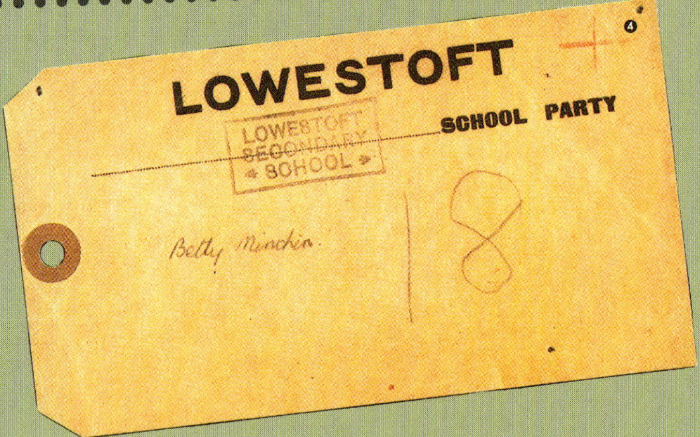

When you arrived in the countryside you were sent to live with a local family. Sometimes local people came to the railway station to "pick" their child to make sure they got one who was clean and tidy.

Many evacuees came from poor families. Sometimes their clothes were scruffy. Some were unwashed and many had head lice and skin diseases.

Some children could not get used to living in a strange place with green fields, sheep and cattle (which they had never seen before). They soon became unhappy and wrote home, begging to go back. Other children really enjoyed their new life in the countryside. Although a few children stayed all through the war, most gradually went back home.

How did the evacuees themselves feel about leaving their parents, to go and live with strangers?

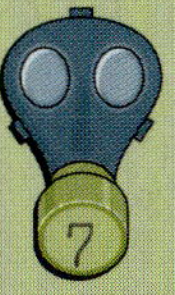

24 Feb 19 4 3

Dear Mummy + Dad,
I am getting rather homesick. Can't you get 2 tickets 1 for Colin + 1 for me to go on the "Clipper" in June? Please do.

I do so much want to come home. There is no danger of invasion now + you say there are very few air-raids + I want to come back. This is not just a homesick fit but it it is real....

SOURCE BOX

Villagers came in to choose children ... We were left until the very last. I sat on my rucksack and cried.

SOURCE BOX

It was like moving to another world and I loved it. I stayed all through the war. The war did change my life.

Some children loved life in the country and stayed there all through the war.

> I have never seen such dirty children. One who came into our shop smelled filthy. Most of them have flea bites all over their bodies.

SOURCE BOX

> A man came to the house and asked how many rooms we had and how many people lived here. I told him, 'Five rooms and three people.' He said, 'Good. You can take two evacuees.'

London County Council

Education Officer's Department,
The County Hall,
Westminster Bridge, S.E.1.
19th March, 1940.

Reference—N

The assembly point for your party is:—

Tottenham Road

The party No. is L.C.C./Plan IV /:—

196

DEAR SIR, OR MADAM,

THE GOVERNMENT'S EVACUATION SCHEME
PLAN IV

1. INTRODUCTION

An important circular recently issued to local authorities by the Ministry of Health sets out the present policy of the Government in regard to evacuation. The policy may be summarised as follows :—

(i) The dispersal of children from the evacuating areas is as desirable now as it was at the outbreak of war.

(ii) It is a vital part of the war effort to encourage the retention in the receiving areas of those children who are already there.

(iii) A plan is to be made for a further evacuation of school children, on the understanding that the plan will be carried into effect only if air raids develop " on a scale involving serious and continuing perils to civilian population."

(iv) Children evacuated under these arrangements will travel in organised parties under the charge of teachers from some or all of the evacuating areas of the country. The Government will decide when the plan for the Metropolitan evacuating area shall be put into operation.

2. METROPOLITAN EVACUATING AREA

The London County Council has been asked to make transport arrangements for certain neighbouring areas in addition to the County of London. They are Acton, Barking, Barnes (part), Brentford and Chiswick, Chingford, Croydon, Dagenham, Ealing (part), East Ham, Edmonton, Enfield (part), Hornchurch (part), Hornsey, Ilford, Leyton, Merton and Morden (part), Mitcham (part), Thurrock (part), Tottenham, Waltham Holy Cross (part), Walthamstow, Wanstead and Woodford, West Ham, Willesden, Wimbledon, Wood Green.

3. ASSEMBLY

The Government's new scheme is known as Plan IV. Those whose evacuation is contemplated under this plan are school children—those who were at school last July or have reached the age of five

22,000 (APC. 41422 15B)—18.3.40—1072

UNDER ATTACK

When the air raids started, the bombs were not spreading gas. Instead there were high explosive bombs that blew up buildings, or *incendiary bombs* that started huge fires.

SOURCE BOX

" Since the bombing started they have all slept in their Anderson shelter, the mother and child on a mattress, the father on a deckchair with cushions and blankets. "

SOURCE BOX

“When the bombs came we went to the underground train station. If you came late the best places would be gone. There would be nothing left except some space at the top of the stairs. Not very safe.”

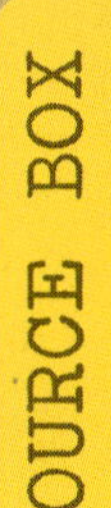

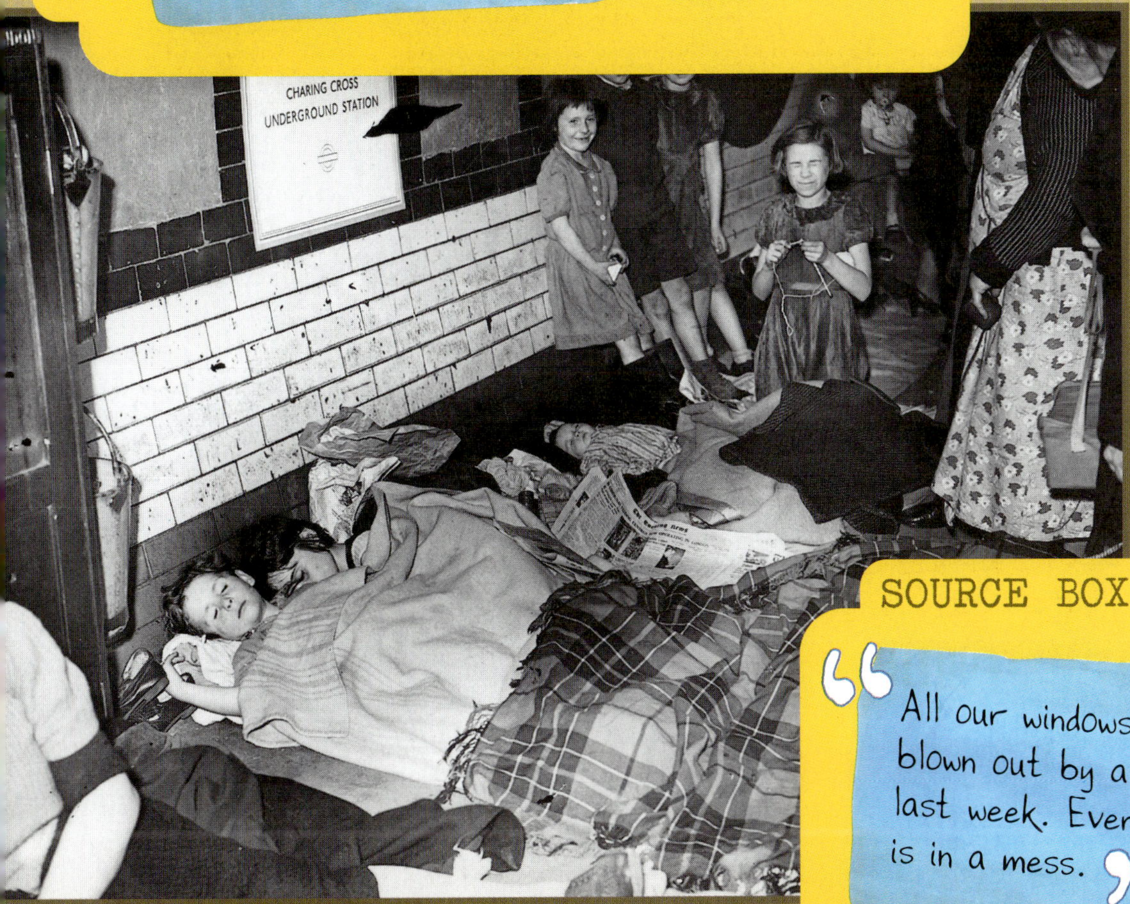

SOURCE BOX

“All our windows were blown out by a bomb last week. Everything is in a mess.”

Night after night, people stayed in an air raid shelter. Many had an Anderson shelter in the back garden. They were always cold and damp. If you did not have your own shelter you went to the nearest public shelter. In London the underground railway (Tube) stations were popular shelters.

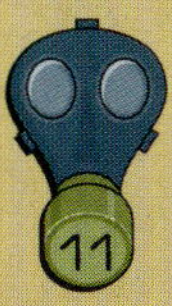

Sometimes **looting** took place after an air raid. People said, "Why leave it for somebody else to pinch? I'm having it."

Coming out of your shelter after a raid you never knew what you would see. The biggest worry was always "Is my house still there?"

If your home had gone you went to stay in a Rest Centre (often part of a school), or friends or relations took you in until you could find somewhere else to live.

How did people's behaviour change with the threat of bombing raids hanging over them?

Many churches were used as Rest Centres during the war.

Rest Centres provided a home for a while if you found that yours had been destroyed in the bombing.

You could leave your door open when the air raid sirens sounded and rush to the shelters to find everything was still there when you returned.

THE BLACKOUT

Posters were created to remind people what they needed to do during blackout times.

The government ordered a "blackout" so that no lights would be seen by enemy planes at night.

What difference did this make to the lives of ordinary people?

You had to make sure that no light from your house could be seen outside. If any light did show, the Air Raid Precautions (ARP) warden would bang on your door, shouting "Turn that light out!"

If your curtains or blinds weren't thick enough, you had to fix cardboard or thick brown paper to the window frame with drawing pins.

At work they have covered all the office windows with brown paper. The only way we can see to work is with the windows wide open or with the lights turned on all day.

Arthur called in to see us with a plaster on his head. In the blackout on Saturday night he had tripped up the kerb, hitting his head on the wall.

Ponies in the New Forest were painted with white stripes, like zebras, so that car drivers would be able to see them more easily. Later the ponies were moved to a safer place.

Outside there were no street lights. Cars had their headlights almost completely covered over, leaving just a small strip of light that was hardly enough to see by. Anybody who broke the blackout rules was likely to end up in court. You could be fined just for striking a match outside at night.

No lights were allowed on the railway stations. Making sure you got off at the right station was not easy.

The number of accidents increased. People were injured walking into lamp posts or even into other people. Several people fell into canals and drowned. Cars often crashed in the dark.

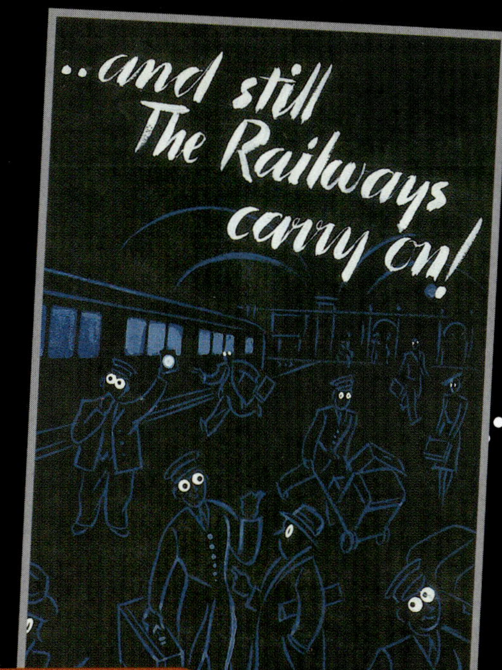

SOURCE BOX

In 1940 a new dance called "The Blackout Stroll" became very popular. During the dance the lights would go out and everybody changed partners in the dark.

WOMEN AT WORK

As men joined the army, navy and air force, women had to take their places at work. It was now important to make extra things needed for the war. Women had to make guns, tanks, planes and ammunition. More food was needed, so women were also needed for farm work.

SOURCE BOX

We started work in the factory. I used to tie a scarf round my head, like a turban, so that my hair wouldn't get caught in the machinery.

SOURCE BOX

My job was to drive a crane. It was better than working inside the factory. The blackout on the windows kept the heat in and it was so hot in there you could hardly breathe.

The hardest work was in the factories. Hours were long, often 70 hours a week, and the work could be dirty and boring. Working in the ammunition factories was dangerous (there were often explosions).

Factory canteens were opened so that workers could get a hot meal. A new wireless programme, *Music While You Work*, was broadcast over factory loudspeakers twice a day so that workers could sing along while they worked. At least you were paid well for working in factories like these.

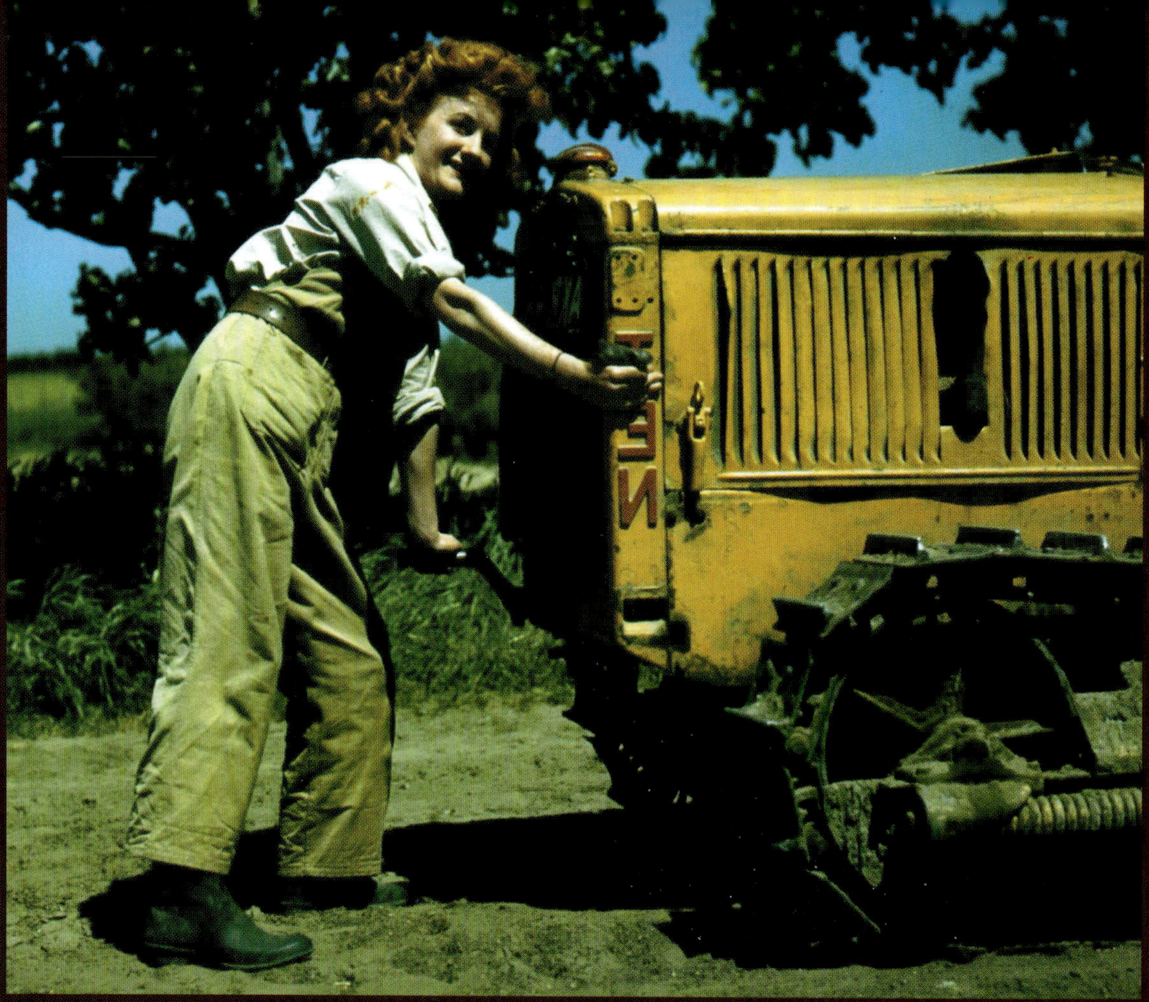

Some women joined the Women's Land Army and went off to work on farms around the country. Although working in the countryside seemed better than working in a factory, the hours were long, pay was low, and the work was often tough and dirty.

How did women adjust to the new demands on them?

SOURCE BOX

"We worked on the farm from six in the morning until ten at night."

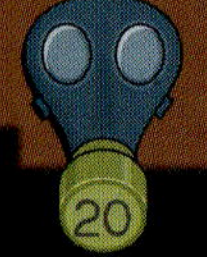

> I enjoyed milking the cows and feeding the hens but I hated cleaning out the henhouses. The dust got everywhere and you got covered in little red insects.

MINISTRY OF AGRICULTURE AND FISHERIES
WOMEN'S LAND ARMY

Surrey _County Secretary_

Address Education Office, Park Street, Guildford.

Telephone No. : Guildford 2053/4

Dear Miss Lang,

NOTIFICATION OF TRAINING

A four weeks' training in hand and machine milking starting on Monday, 11th May 1942 has been arranged for you, as a member of the Women's Land Army, with Dauntsey School at West Lavington, Devizes

During training you will be billeted at Mrs. Andrews, Spin Hill, Market Lavington, Devizes

The nearest station is Lavington

You should arrive on Monday, 11th May 1942 Please notify of the time of your arrival as soon as possible.

[P.T.O.

6.—**Sickness or Accident.**—Directly you arrive at your place of training obtain a Medical Card from the nearest Post Office if you have not one already and arrange to have your name entered on the Health Insurance Panel of a nearby doctor. **Do not wait to do this until you are ill.**

If you are unable to continue your training on account of illness or accident, call in your panel doctor and tell your County Secretary at once. You will not receive any Personal Allowance during your period of incapacity. If you are able to do so you should return home and you may then apply for a refund of your travelling expenses.

MAKE DO AND MEND

Before the war a lot of the food eaten in Britain came from abroad. Ships still tried to bring in food from other countries.

But many of the ships were sunk by German submarines. The country had to grow more food or people would go hungry.

Gardens, parks and school fields were dug up and used to grow potatoes and other vegetables. Many people kept hens or a pig in the back garden.

There was still not enough food to go round. The answer was to introduce rationing. If an item of food was rationed, you were allowed to buy only a small amount of it each week. Not all foods were rationed but the list gradually became longer. Bacon, ham, butter, sugar, meat, tea, margarine, cheese, jam, syrup, treacle, marmalade, eggs, rice, biscuits, sweets and chocolate were all rationed. Rabbit meat became very popular for a while but soon even this was difficult to find.

It was not only food that was
in short supply. Other things
such as petrol, coal, soap and
clothes were also rationed.
The shortages meant people
had to "make do and mend".

Recycling was important during the
war. Anything from old clothes to
pots and pans were used to make
vehicles and weapons.

24

Everyone was ordered not to waste anything whether it was food, paper (for recycling) or old rags (these could be recycled into uniforms and blankets).

How did rationing affect people?

GOING TO SCHOOL

How did going to school change during the war?

In many country areas the arrival of children evacuated from the towns meant that the village school was not big enough. Lessons often took place in other buildings – in private houses or church halls. Often there were not enough teachers.

This became worse as the war went on and more and more male teachers went to war. Sometimes 50 or 60 children were taught in one classroom by one teacher. Often the only answer was to have part-time school. Some children went to school in the morning only and the rest in the afternoon.

11th January 1941. Two children are not here because of unexploded bombs in the fields they come through. Police are there.

Schools also had to "make do and mend". Pencils were in short supply and had to be shared. Because of the paper shortage, reading books could not be replaced no matter how badly they were falling apart. (There was one good thing. Because you had to save paper, you were asked to do less written work!)

SOURCE BOX

12th March 1941. This morning at play-time I took the children to see two bomb craters. Five bombs fell around the village but they all fell in the fields.

SOURCE BOX

In 1941 the Head Teacher of a school in London wrote that the school had taken over a piece of waste land nearby. In one year the children had grown piles of potatoes and lots of green vegetables.

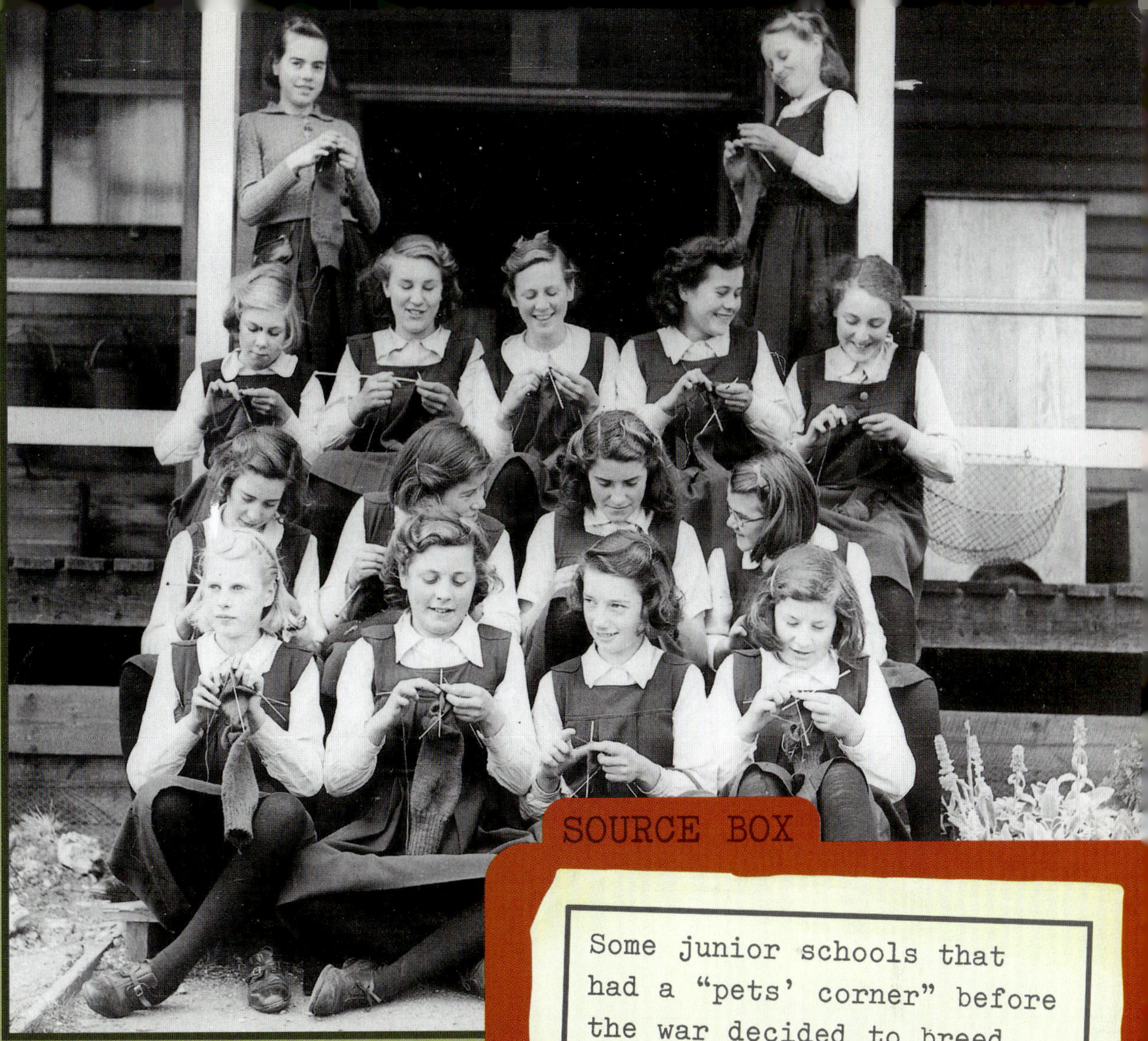

Some junior schools that had a "pets' corner" before the war decided to breed rabbits instead to provide extra food.

There were some differences in school lessons. The main one was that schools were often now starting to "dig for victory" so agriculture, gardening and even keeping animals became school lessons. Some lessons, like woodwork and cooking, stopped because of the shortages of wood and food.

PEACE AT LAST

On 8th May 1945, the Prime Minister, Winston Churchill, told the country that "The German war is at an end." Everybody celebrated. Union Jack flags were flying out of bedroom windows and from lamp posts.

Winston Churchill

Street parties were held across the country to celebrate Victory in Europe Day (VE Day).

People danced in the street.
There were parties everywhere.
But some things had changed for ever.
- Now more and more married women carried on working.
- Old houses in town centres which had been bombed were replaced by new houses built outside the towns.
- Many children would grow up in families where fathers had been killed in the fighting.

Things would never be quite the same again.

GLOSSARY

agriculture farming

ammunition bullets, shells and grenades

Anderson shelter an air raid shelter made of curved sheets of corrugated iron covering a hole in the ground

evacuated moved from a dangerous place to a safe place

evacuee someone who had been evacuated

fined made to pay money as a punishment

incendiary bomb explosive device, designed to cause fires

looting stealing from houses or shops

rationing a system to make sure everyone had a small amount of essential foods each week

Union Jack the red, white and blue flag of the United Kingdom

wireless radio

INDEX